The Great
Big
Brain
Book

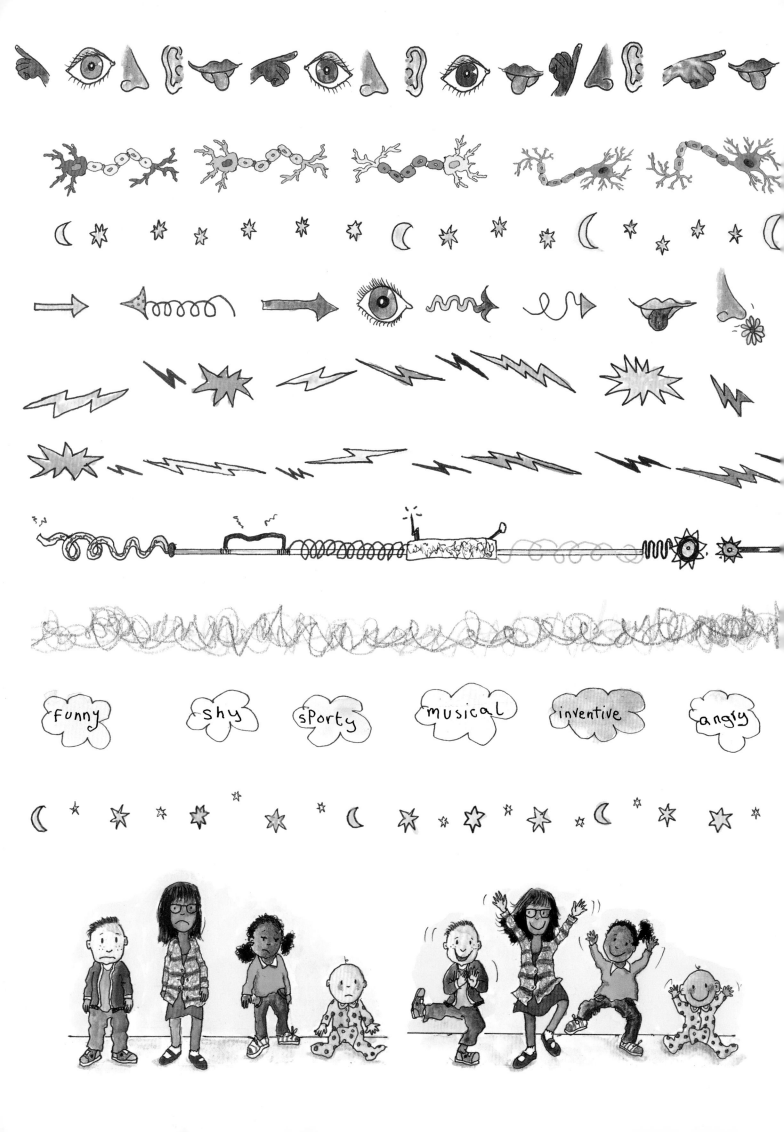

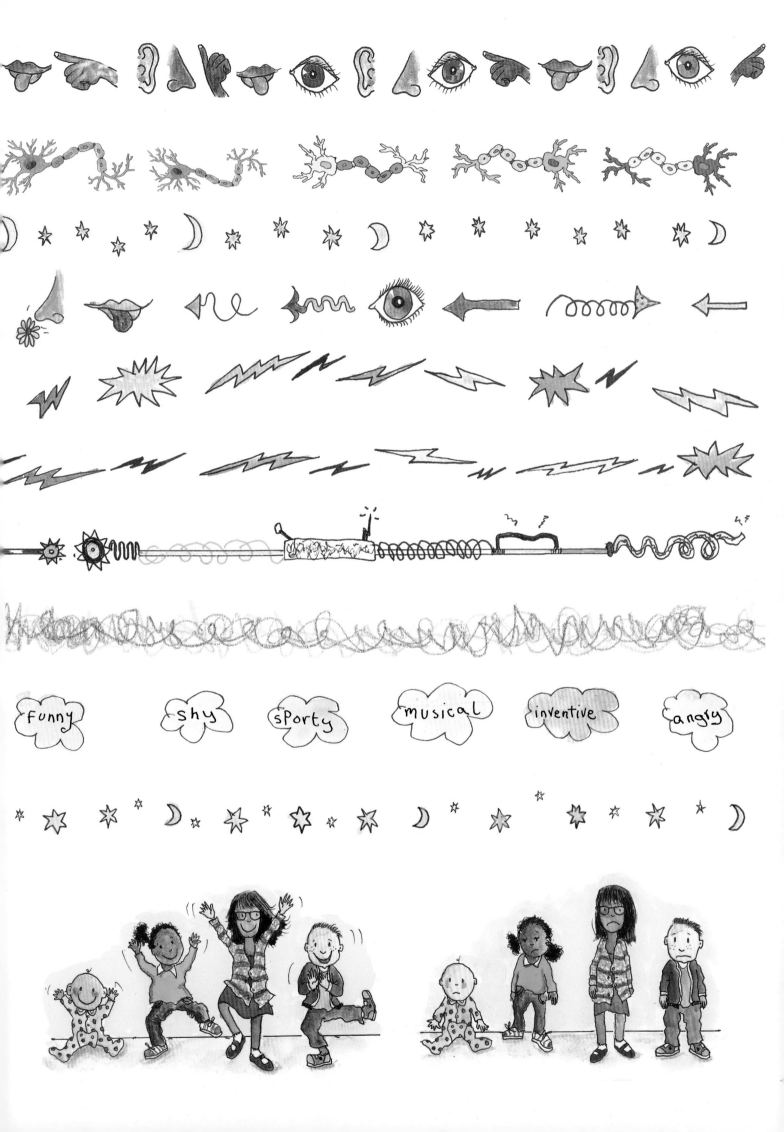

For Joseph and Leo Lloyd-Mostyn – MH
For Theo and Olympia, with love– RA

The publishers and authors would like to thank Dr Peter Boers
for his invaluable advice and support as consultant for this book.

The Great Big Brain Book © 2020 Quarto Publishing plc.
Text © 2020 Mary Hoffman. Illustrations © 2020 Ros Asquith.

First Published in 2020 by Frances Lincoln Children's Books, an imprint of The Quarto Group.
This paperback edition first published in 2021
The Old Brewery, 6 Blundell Street, London N7 9BH, United Kingdom.
T (0)20 7700 6700 F (0)20 7700 8066 www.QuartoKnows.com

A catalogue record for this book is available from the British Library.

ISBN 978-0-7112-4155-8

The illustrations were created with watercolours
Set in Green

Published by Rachel Williams
Designed by Judith Escreet
Edited by Claire Grace
Production by Nicolas Zeifman

Manufactured in Guangdong, China EB112020

9 8 7 6 5 4 3 2 1

The Great Big Brain Book

Can you find ME every time you turn a page?

Mary Hoffman and Ros Asquith

Frances Lincoln
Children's Books

YOUR AMAZING BRAIN

Brains are amazing! They are in charge of every single thing our bodies can do.

Just think of all the things you wouldn't be able to do without your brain – walking, talking, thinking, feeling, not to mention your lungs moving in and out so you can breathe and your heart beating as it sends blood round your body.

You wouldn't be able to learn or remember anything
or have any new ideas. No-one would ever invent
anything or write a book or paint a picture or
be able to play a musical instrument.
In fact, we wouldn't be able to do anything at all
without our brains.

The COMMAND centre

Our brains have been compared to computers because they process information.
And to the universe because they are so complicated.

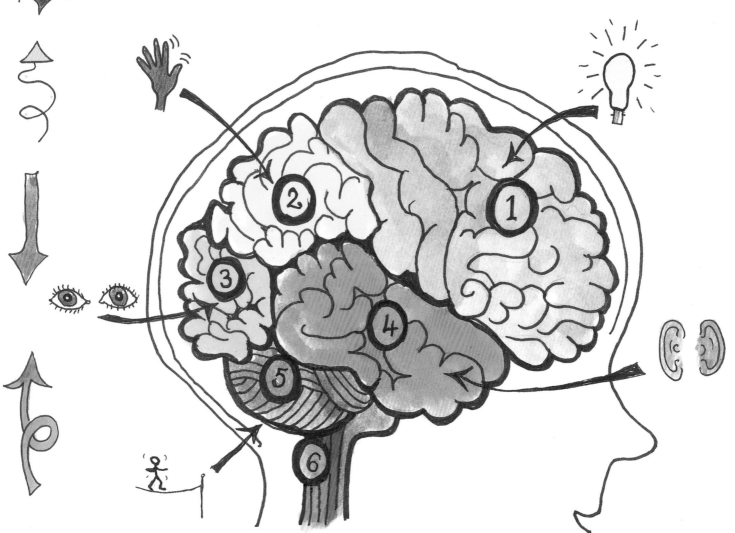

① Movement, memory, language, behaviour

② Reading, touch, sensation

③ Sight

④ Memory, language, hearing

⑤ Balance

⑥ Connects the brain to the spinal cord

Some say our brains are like a factory because they make so many things. Or like a spider's web because of their complex structure. Or even like a city, where everything does what it is supposed to on most days – a miracle of organisation!

Let's think of it as a control room or command centre, sending and receiving messages to and from all parts of the body.

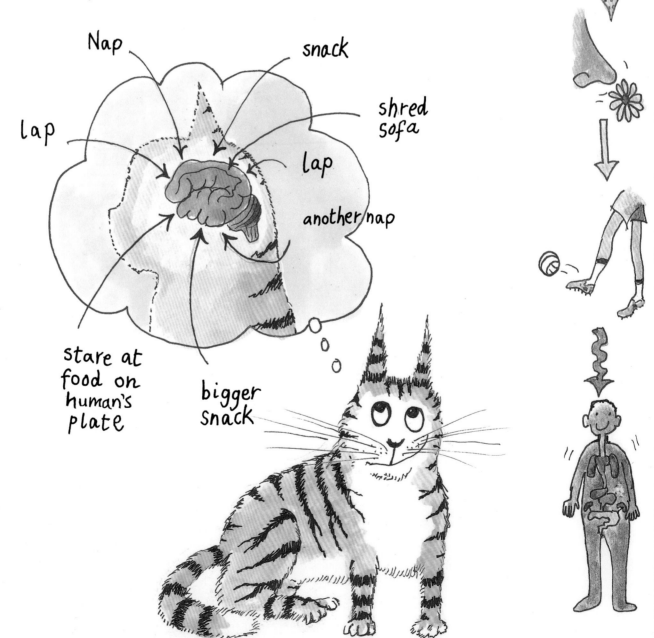

Nap

snack

shred sofa

lap

lap

another nap

stare at food on human's plate

bigger snack

YOUR GROWING BRAIN

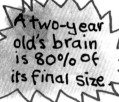

A brain weighs over 1 kg!

Your brain sits inside your skull, the hard bony covering you can feel all over your head. It protects the brain from injury and accidents.

A two-year old's brain is 80% of its final size.

Your brain started to develop before you were born, in the first few weeks you were growing in your mother's body. It was fully formed by the time you had been there six or seven months.

The brain is 2% of a human's body weight.

Humans can make fresh brain cells into their 90s.

There are 86 billion nerve cells in your brain.

A whale's brain is five times heavier than a human's.

But your brain goes on developing for years and depends on your eating good food, taking exercise and being well looked after.

75% of your brain is WATER.

BRAin FOOD

Nuts

Vegetables

Fruit

Wholemeal BREAd and pasta

Oily Fish + eggs

I've lost over 1 kg! Hope it's not my brain.

A cat's brain only weighs 28 grams

By the time you are six years old your brain is almost fully developed but it changes again a lot during teenage years.

The SENSES

One of the brain's jobs is to send messages around our bodies to reach our nervous system, using tiny cells called neurons, and to receive messages back. So, if you *touch* something, the neurons head back to your brain to say if it's hard or soft, hot or cold, rough or smooth, or a range of other things – sticky, furry, slimy, prickly.

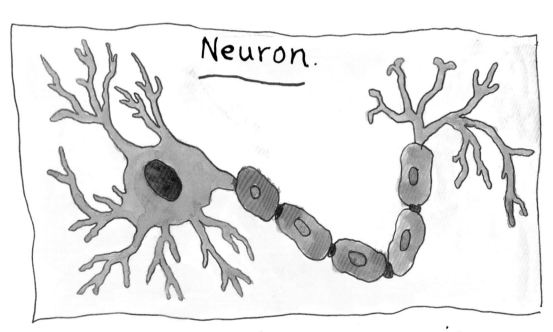

Neuron.

It's like an alien from outer space.

Or a spider crossed with a caterpillar.

And it's the same with the other four senses: *smell*, *sight*, *hearing* and *taste*.

Neurons also send back messages to our brains about pain and whether our body is too hot or too cold. They help us to keep our balance when we stand, walk, ride a bike or balance on a gym bar.

And all these things are done so quickly that we don't even have to think about them.

WALKING & TALKING

Our brains control the muscles, bones and tendons that allow us to move our arms and legs. Small children have to learn how to use all these things together so that they can learn to walk. It's the same when we talk – we have to learn to use our breath and our tongues, teeth and vocal cords.

The brain allows us to do all kinds of fiddly and difficult things with our hands and arms, from picking up small things to carving tiny sculptures.

When the messages get a bit scrambled you might be clumsy and drop or spill things.

Your neurons are playing up!

THINKING and LEARNING

Different parts of the brain allow us to learn and understand different things. But it's hard to say which part creates ideas or where your imagination sits in the brain.

  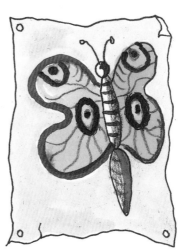 

We can think about what we know and make decisions. We can plan something like a journey or solve problems.

Many people can do several things at once because their brains let them organise their thoughts and movements so well.

POLISH

HOW are YOU FEELING?

Our feelings, whether we are happy or sad, excited or bored, angry or calm, all come from somewhere in our brains. You may feel happy and excited thinking about something fun you are going to do at the weekend or sad because your dog isn't very well or angry because your teacher thought you had done something bad when you hadn't.

But all those thoughts go through your brain and cause your reactions to them.

And our brains can be trained to have different feelings – we can learn to control what we feel.

You can be sad one minute—

And happy the next.

TAIL WAGGING

Angry   Happy

BLAH

 # LANGUAGE

 yak

 yak

We learn to talk because our brains help us hear what other people say - often our parents first. Our brains teach our mouths to make lots of sounds, which are mostly just babbling and nonsense when we are very small.

 Blah

 BLAH

 Yak

Blah Yak Yakkety-yak Blah Yak Yak

 Blah

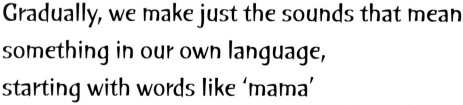 Adults are not always listening.

Gradually, we make just the sounds that mean something in our own language, starting with words like 'mama' and 'dada' or 'more' and 'bang!' Learning to read or write words comes later.

 yak

 Yak-Yak

 There's one word I ALWAYS hear. DINNER!

But what if you are born without being able to hear? Then you may learn sign language, which also involves your brain to make the signs and understand them.

And if you are blind, you might learn to read braille, a system of raised dots on pages, for which of course you need your brain just as much, to help you understand them.

Remember, remember!

One of the most important things your brain does is to remember things. Some things that you learn, like walking, don't need you to think about them any more – you just do them. But the memory of HOW to do them is somewhere deep inside your brain.

It's the same when grown-ups learn to drive a car or play the piano.

One hundred years ago, grandpa was born. (JOKE!)

Six years ago, I was born. I can't remember that, but grandpa can.

Let's stroll down memory lane.

Two years ago Theo was born.

One year ago I was five.

Twelve hours ago I was asleep.

Five minutes ago I put on my coat to go out with grandpa.

We can store memories like pictures in a photo album. They can be good or bad, happy or sad.

But for some people, who have had a stroke or have an illness that affects memory, called Alzheimer's, memory goes a bit wrong. They can remember things that happened ages ago, when they were children, but not what happened yesterday.

And some people can 'lose' parts of their memory altogether. This is called amnesia and can be the result of an accident.

SLEEPING & DREAMING

When we go to sleep, our bodies don't switch off. Instead, they sort of 'power down'. Our brains keep working while our cells are refreshed and renewed by having a good, long rest.

When we are deeply asleep, our brains give us dreams. These can be very lifelike and sometimes peculiar! They can be lovely happy images of being by the sea or in a magical jungle.

Or they can be horrible nightmares about being chased and eaten by monsters.

No-one knows exactly why we have dreams and what they are for. Maybe it is all part of recharging our brain and getting rid of things we don't need.

ENERGY

Along with many other things, your brain controls your energy levels. The brain itself uses a quarter of all the glucose in your body, which is the main source of energy. If our brains don't get enough glucose, we may faint or have problems concentrating. This is one of the reasons it is so important to have a good breakfast.

This is what can happen to people who have diabetes. They need to be sure to eat regularly and take their medicine, so that their bodies have the right level of glucose to function, especially their brains.

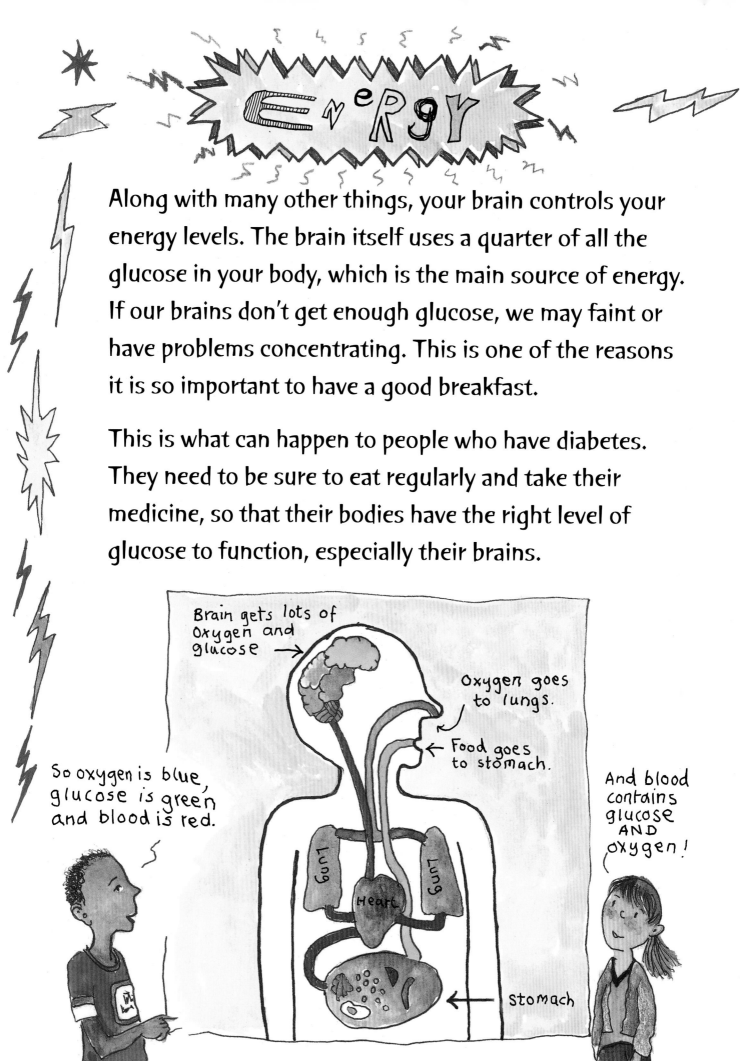

Brain gets lots of oxygen and glucose →

Oxygen goes to lungs.

← Food goes to stomach.

So oxygen is blue, glucose is green and blood is red.

And blood contains glucose AND oxygen!

Lung

Lung

Heart

Stomach ←

Our brains tell us when we are too hot or too cold and can help us by sweating or giving us goose bumps.

When you think of all the things your brain does, it's not surprising it uses a lot of energy! Our brains tell us when we need to eat or drink and when we need to visit the loo. Or when we've had enough to eat and when we are tired and need to sleep.

I'm not lazy, just low on glucose.

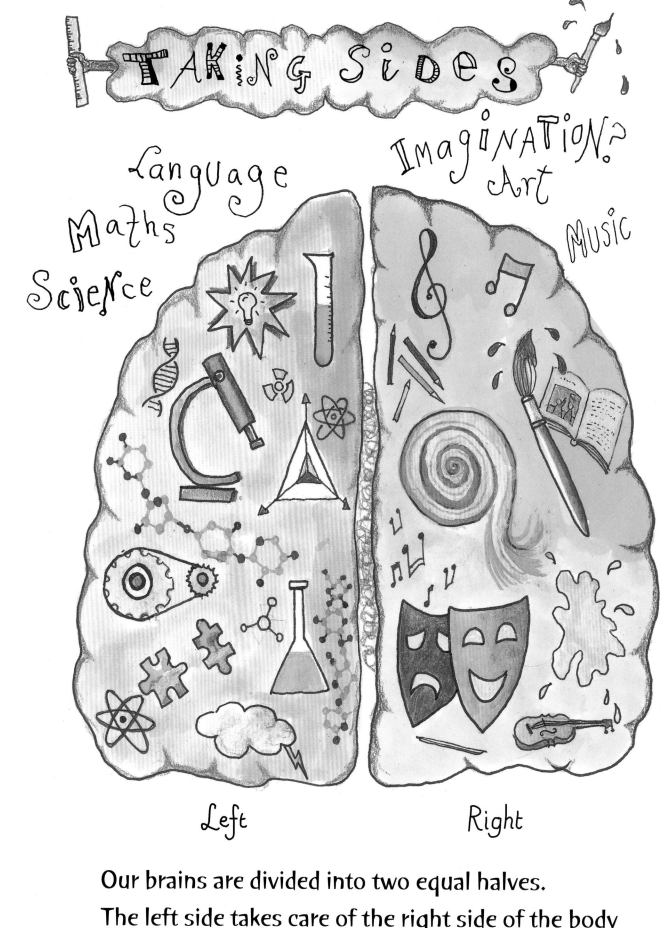

TAKING SIDES

Language

Maths

Science

Imagination?

Art

Music

Left

Right

Our brains are divided into two equal halves.
The left side takes care of the right side of the body
and the right side looks after the left side of the body.
No-one knows exactly why this happens.

The left front part of our brains is specially involved with language, maths and scientific facts. The right side is supposed to respond to art and music and may even be where our imagination comes from.

I hear music is wonderful for left/right brain coordination.

Pat pat

Rub rub

WHeN BRAINS are DIFFEReNT

My brain may be different, but there are lots of things I do really well.

Sometimes brains develop differently and then people may have epilepsy (fits) or autism. Or an accident can cause brain damage, meaning that any of the many, many things a brain does can go wrong.

Sometimes a brain develops a tumour – a fleshy growth that can appear anywhere in the brain. The tumour presses on nerves and gives us terrible headaches and causes many other problems.

For older people some things that give their brains problems are dementia and Alzheimer's. They can also have strokes – caused by developing blood clots on the brain or bleeding in part of the brain. All of these things can cause people's memories to fail or other things to stop working.

I may not remember your name, but I can still have a good laugh!

Sometimes they can no longer recognise members of their families and their personalities may change. This is terribly sad for the people who love them.

ARTIFICIAL INTELLIGENCE

You may have heard someone say 'AI', which stands for 'Artificial Intelligence'. That makes us think of robots – machines who look a bit like people. But what it does is to behave a bit like a human brain, using computers to learn information and follow rules. Systems like this can recognise speech or be given enough information to solve problems. AI lies behind ideas like driverless cars, which might be what all people have in the future.

But our brains help us do **ALL** those things, and much **MORE!**

HOORAY for BRAINS!

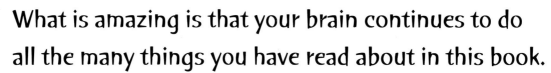

What is amazing is that your brain continues to do all the many things you have read about in this book.

Your intelligence and personality come from your brain. All the things that make you different from anybody else started in your brain.

Your personality, interests and abilities also depend on who your parents were, how you were brought up and the love and care you receive.

 shy

 sporty

 musical

 inventive

 kind

But whether you are left or right-handed, how well you can solve problems, how much you like being with other people or prefer being on your own, whether you like to read or play games or are good at sport are all the result of how your body and brain interact.

Long live brains! What would we do without them?

 acrobatic

creative

Some Useful Words

Alzheimer's disease

An illness which usually affects old people, which causes them to lose their memory. It is caused by damage to brain cells and is a form of dementia.

Amnesia

The loss of all memory. Sometimes it comes back after a while.

Asperger's syndrome

A form of autism. People with Asperger's syndrome may find difficulty in social relationships and in communicating.

Autism

People with autism may have difficulty interacting with others, and see, hear and feel the world differently from others.

Dementia

There are several kinds of dementia but they all involve loss of memory, confusion, having difficulty with communication and losing normal sense of time.

Epilepsy

Can be a result of brain damage before birth or much later in life. It results in having a type of fit in which the epileptic person goes stiff and then loses control of their limbs.

Neuron

A cell that carries messages to and from the brain and also within the brain.

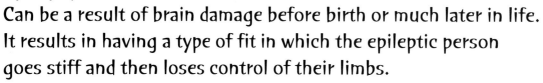

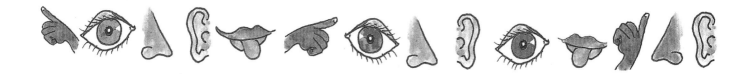

Nervous system
The network of neurons transmitting impulses between parts of the brain and body.

Senses
How our bodies recognise what's happening in the outside world – sight, hearing, smell, taste and touch.

Skull
The hard, bony part of your head that protects your brain.

Spinal cord
The bundle of nerves running inside our spines that carries information to and from all parts of the body.

Stroke
An illness in which the blood supply to part of the brain is stopped. It may be caused by a blood clot or by bleeding. If not treated quickly, it can result in brain damage.

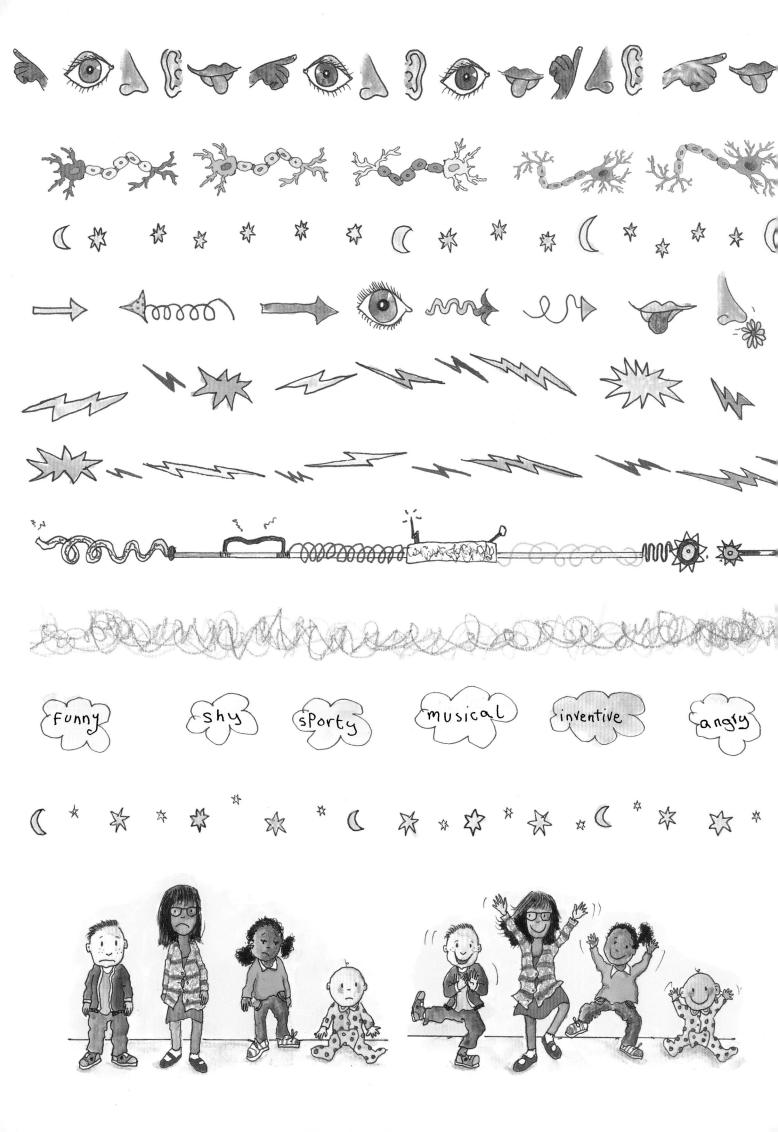

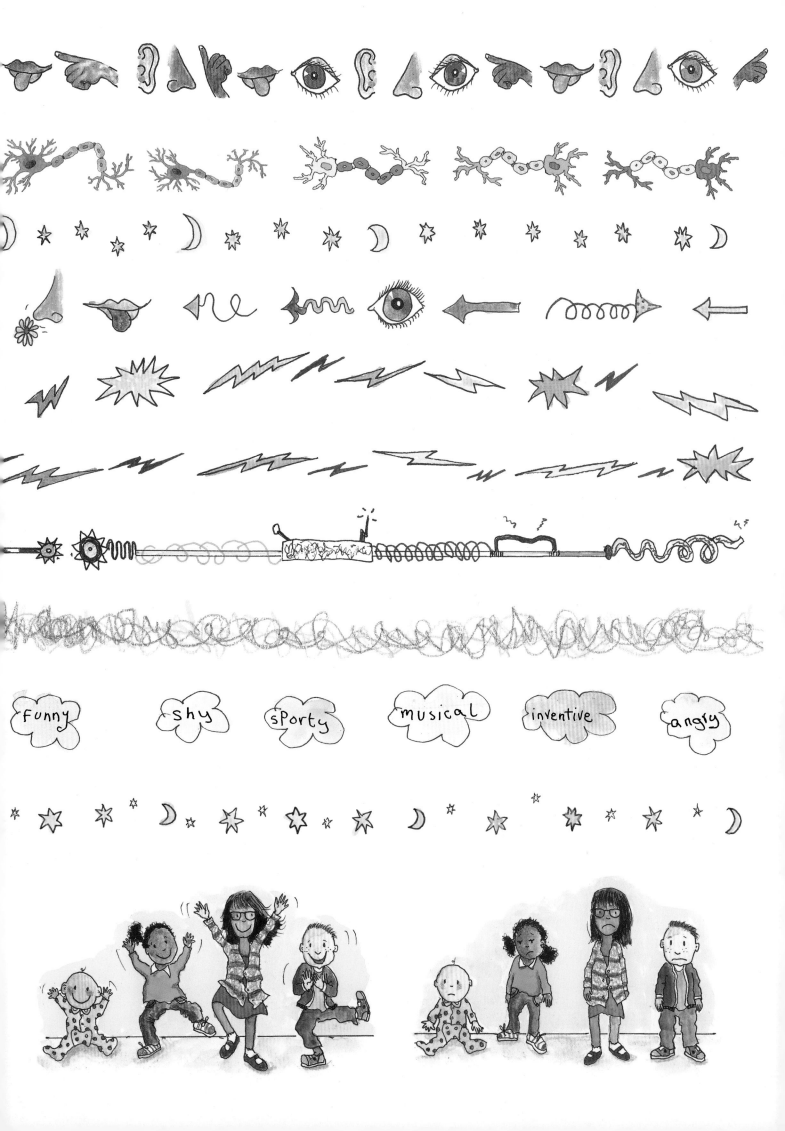

ALSO IN THE GREAT BIG BOOK SERIES,
BY MARY HOFFMAN AND ROS ASQUITH:

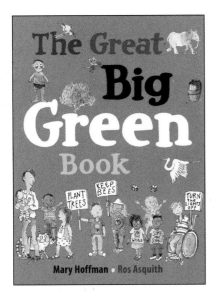

The Great Big Green Book

The eco-friendly guide to helping save the planet that all young children can learn from.

978-1-78603-095-5

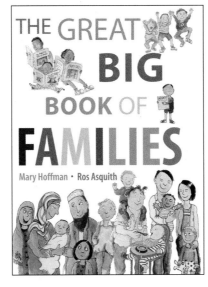

The Great Big Book of Families

A fresh, optimistic look through children's eyes at today's wide variety of families.

978-1-84780-587-4

The Great Big Book of Feelings

This book celebrates each emotion for what it is and encourages children to discuss how they're feeling.

978-1-84780-758-8

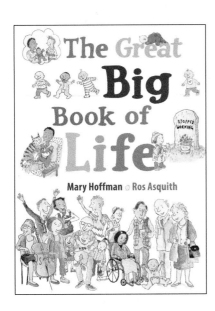

The Great Big Book of Life

A diverse celebration of human life, from birth to death, featuring funny artwork and sensitive text.

978-1-78603-180-8

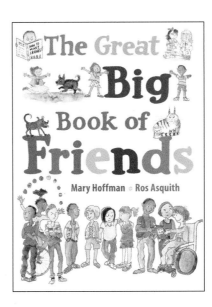

The Great Big Book of Friends

A wonderfully accessible and inclusive book about every kind of friendship.

978-1-78603-666-7

The Great Big Body Book

Birth, growth, ageing, senses, the brain and genetics are all covered in this unique exploration of the human body.

978-1-84780-686-4